BIANKA KLOCKO

DOG BREEDING BUSINESS FOR BEGINNERS

A Comprehensive Guide to Ethical Dog Breeding Practices, Business Management, and Responsible Dog Ownership

DEDICATION

To the tireless dreamers and compassionate caretakers, this book is dedicated to those who find purpose in the wag of a tail, the joy of new life, and the commitment to ethical stewardship. May your journey in dog breeding be filled with fulfillment, and may your dedication echo in the paws that leave lasting imprints on the hearts of families. This is for the dogs, the breeders, and the shared love that unites us all.

Contents

Chapter 1

Welcome to the captivating realm of dog breeding, a world where passion meets responsibility, and the bond between humans and dogs is forged with care and commitment. In your pursuit of becoming a dog breeder, this guide stands as your trusted companion—a roadmap to navigate the intricacies of ethical breeding practices, effective business management, and the profound responsibilities that accompany the role.

An Oath to Ethical Breeding:

At the heart of every responsible dog breeder lies a deep commitment to ethical principles. Within these pages, we explore the essence of ethical practices, unveiling the core values that underpin a breeder's dedication. This journey distinguishes between responsible and irresponsible practices, emphasizing principles that safeguard the health and well-being of both parent dogs and their offspring.

Traversing the Genetic Landscape:

Embark on a voyage into the intricate world of breed standards and genetic health. Discover the significance of adhering to breed standards, steering clear of genetic pitfalls, and unraveling the fascinating complexities of dog genetics. This knowledge empowers you to make informed breeding pairings, preserving the integrity of each breed while ensuring the health and vitality of future generations.

Fostering Excellence in Breeding Programs:

The success of your breeding program hinges on the health and well-being of your dogs. Learn to establish a program that prioritizes nutrition, exercise, wellness, and a safe, clean breeding environment. Picture a haven where responsible breeding practices thrive, creating an environment where dogs flourish and the bond between breeder and canine companion is nurtured.

Crafting Your Breeder's Identity:

Ethical breeding extends beyond the kennel; it resonates in every interaction with potential puppy parents. Explore responsible advertising and marketing, emphasizing ethical promotion and building a positive reputation. Discover how to leverage digital platforms to share your commitment to responsible breeding practices with a wider audience.

Navigating the Business Landscape:

To be the ethical breeder you aspire to become, understanding the legal landscape is paramount. Uncover the intricacies of legal requirements and regulatory compliance for dog breeders. Armed with this knowledge, navigate the business terrain with confidence, ensuring your practices align with ethical standards and legal obligations.

Building the Foundation of Success:

Delve into the development of a comprehensive business plan, covering financial projections, budgeting, and effective marketing and sales strategies. Envision a roadmap that leads not only to financial sustainability but also to a thriving community of responsible dog breeders.

From Conception to Companion:
Celebrate the entire journey of responsible dog ownership and puppy care. Explore realms of prenatal and postnatal care, socialization, training, and nutrition for puppies. Identify and address potential health issues, and learn to educate new puppy owners about responsible dog ownership. This section is a celebration of the lifelong companionship between a dog and its human family.

A Holistic Approach to Breeding Excellence:
Consider additional considerations and resources—from choosing the right breed to maintaining accurate pedigrees, collaborating with professionals, and staying informed about ethical concerns. This reservoir of knowledge is designed to guide you through every facet of your journey.

As you embark on this literary adventure, keep in mind that knowledge is dynamic. Regularly update and revise your understanding, reflecting changes in regulations, best practices, and industry trends. Together, let's ensure that your journey in the realm of ethical dog breeding is both enriching and enduring.

Are you ready to delve into the depths of ethical breeding practices and foster excellence in your dog breeding journey?

Brief History

Exploring the history of dog breeding is a fascinating journey that spans thousands of years, shaped by the intricate relationship between humans and canines. Let's unravel the historical tapestry of dog breeding.

Ancient Beginnings: The history of dog breeding dates back to ancient times when humans and wolves formed an alliance. As early hunter-gatherers settled into agricultural communities, they recognized the utility of wolves in activities such as hunting, herding, and guarding. This mutual cooperation marked the inception of intentional dog breeding.

Selective Breeding in Antiquity: Civilizations like the Egyptians, Greeks, and Romans were among the first to engage in selective breeding. Dogs were bred for specific purposes, such as hunting, guarding, and companionship. Notably, ancient Romans valued specific breeds for their unique traits, contributing to the diversity we see in modern dog breeds.

The Middle Ages: During the Middle Ages, distinct breeds began to emerge as societies became more structured. Nobility and royalty were particularly keen on breeding dogs for companionship and as status symbols. Breeds like the Greyhound and Mastiff were highly esteemed, each serving specific functions in the aristocratic lifestyle.

The Renaissance and the Rise of Dog Shows: The Renaissance witnessed a renewed interest in the arts and sciences, including the systematic study of dog breeds. Dog shows became popular in the 19th century, further shaping the concept of breed standards and conformation. The Kennel Club in the United Kingdom, established in 1873, played a pivotal role in formalizing breed standards and organizing dog shows.

Industrial Revolution and Urbanization: The Industrial Revolution brought about significant social changes, leading to increased urbanization. This shift influenced the types of dogs people desired, with smaller breeds becoming popular in urban settings. The Victorian era saw the emergence of many recognizable breeds like the Dachshund and Poodle.

World Wars and Post-War Era: The World Wars had profound effects on dog breeding. Some breeds faced near extinction due to wartime conditions. However, the post-war era saw a resurgence, with renewed interest in preserving and promoting various breeds. The mid-20th century witnessed the formal establishment of breed clubs and kennel associations globally.

Modern Era: Today, dog breeding is a dynamic and diverse field. The establishment of kennel clubs, breed standards, and the growing popularity of dog shows contribute to the continued evolution of breeds. Contemporary breeding practices focus on preserving breed integrity, addressing health concerns, and promoting responsible ownership.

As we explore the rich history of dog breeding, it becomes evident that the practice has evolved from a utilitarian partnership to a sophisticated and intentional endeavor. The diversity of dog breeds we cherish today reflects centuries of human ingenuity, collaboration, and a deep appreciation for the unique qualities that make each canine companion special.

Chapter 2

UNDERSTANDING ETHICAL BREEDING

In the intricate world of dog breeding, the foundation of responsible practices begins with a clear understanding of ethics. Ethical breeding is not merely a set of guidelines but a profound commitment to the well-being of dogs and the preservation of their breeds. This chapter seeks to unravel the essence of ethical breeding, starting with the fundamental concept of what it truly means.

Ethics Beyond Boundaries: At its core, ethical breeding transcends the mere adherence to rules; it embodies a commitment to the principles that safeguard the physical and mental health of both parent dogs and their offspring. It's about recognizing the moral responsibility that comes with bringing new life into the world and ensuring that life is lived with dignity and fulfillment.

Respect for Life: Defining ethical breeding involves an unwavering respect for the intrinsic value of each individual dog. It means considering the well-being of the breeding dogs as paramount, understanding that their health and happiness are directly linked to the quality of the breeding program. Ethical breeders prioritize the overall welfare of their canine companions.

Transparency and Integrity: Ethical breeding operates in the light of transparency and integrity. Breeders committed to ethical practices openly share information about their breeding programs, including health records, living conditions, and genetic testing. Transparency builds trust with potential puppy parents and contributes to the responsible and informed selection of breeding pairs.

Breed Preservation: Preserving the integrity of each breed is a cornerstone of ethical breeding. This involves a deep understanding of breed standards and a commitment to maintaining those standards through thoughtful pairings. Ethical breeders contribute to the preservation of breeds, respecting the unique traits and characteristics that define each one.

Responsible Placement of Puppies: Ethical breeding extends beyond the birth of puppies; it encompasses their entire life journey. Responsible placement involves careful consideration of potential homes, ensuring that puppies are matched with families that can provide the necessary care, attention, and commitment to their well-being.

Principles and Core Values

1. **Compassionate Care:** Ethical breeding places the utmost importance on compassionate care for breeding dogs. This involves providing a nurturing environment that prioritizes the physical and emotional well-being of each dog. From proper nutrition to veterinary care and a comfortable living space, compassionate care ensures that breeding dogs lead happy, healthy lives.

2. **Health Screening and Genetic Responsibility:** A commitment to health screening and genetic responsibility is a key principle. Ethical breeders diligently assess the health of breeding dogs through regular check-ups and genetic testing. This proactive approach aims to identify and mitigate potential hereditary issues, contributing to the overall health and longevity of the breed.

3. **Selective Pairing for Breed Standards:** Ethical breeding adheres to breed standards with unwavering dedication. This principle involves thoughtful and selective pairing of breeding dogs to preserve the unique traits and characteristics outlined in breed standards. By upholding these standards, ethical breeders contribute to the continuity of distinct breeds.

4. **Transparency and Open Communication:** Transparency and open communication are core values that underpin ethical breeding. Breeders openly share information about their practices, including health records, breeding history, and living conditions. This transparency fosters trust between breeders and potential puppy owners, creating a foundation for responsible

and informed decisions.

5. *Lifetime Responsibility:* Ethical breeding extends beyond the whelping box; it encompasses a lifetime commitment to each dog produced. Breeders take responsibility for the well-being of their puppies, ensuring they are placed in suitable homes. This commitment includes being a resource for puppy owners, offering guidance and support throughout the dog's life.

6. *Respect for the Individual:* Every dog is unique, and ethical breeding acknowledges and respects this individuality. This principle involves recognizing the inherent value of each dog, regardless of breeding status. Ethical breeders treat their dogs with respect, acknowledging their distinct personalities and needs.

7. *Continuous Education and Improvement:* Ethical breeders are lifelong learners committed to continuous education and improvement. Staying informed about advancements in veterinary care, genetics, and overall dog welfare allows breeders to adapt and enhance their practices over time. This commitment ensures that ethical breeders are at the forefront of positive change within the field.

Differentiating Responsible vs. Irresponsible Practices

Responsible Breeding: Responsible breeding is characterized by a commitment to the well-being of the breeding dogs, the preservation of breed standards, and the ethical treatment of each dog throughout its life. Here are key elements that distinguish responsible breeding practices:

- **Health Screening:** Responsible breeders conduct thorough health screenings for breeding dogs, including genetic testing, regular veterinary check-ups, and proactive measures to address potential health issues.
- **Selective Pairing:** Thoughtful and selective pairing of breeding dogs is a hallmark of responsible breeding. This process adheres to breed standards, aiming to enhance and preserve the unique qualities of the breed.
- **Lifetime Support:** Responsible breeders provide ongoing support to puppy owners, offering guidance, resources, and a commitment to the well-being of each dog produced.

2. *Irresponsible Breeding:* Irresponsible breeding practices often neglect the well-being of breeding dogs and overlook essential aspects of breed preservation. Let us look at the indicators of irresponsible breeding practices:

- **Lack of Health Screening:** Irresponsible breeders may neglect health screenings, leading to the propagation of genetic issues and potential health problems in offspring.
- **Unselective Pairing:** Pairing breeding dogs without consideration for breed standards or genetic compatibility may result in offspring that deviate significantly from the desired traits of the breed.
- **Lack of Support:** Irresponsible breeders may fail to provide adequate support to puppy owners, neglecting the responsibility that extends beyond the initial sale.

Chapter 3

BREED STANDARDS AND GENETIC HEALTH

Adhering to Standards

Preserving the essence of dog breeds involves a deep commitment to adhering to established standards. These standards, meticulously detailing the ideal characteristics, appearance, and temperament of each breed, serve as a guiding compass for ethical breeders.

Understanding the specific traits that define each breed is paramount. Ethical breeders immerse themselves in the intricacies of these standards, recognizing that adherence ensures the unique and identifiable characteristics of a breed are maintained over time.

Selecting breeding pairs becomes a meticulous process. Responsible breeders carefully assess potential mates, seeking compatibility with established standards. This thoughtful selection process aims not only to enhance but also to maintain the desired qualities of the breed, fostering consistency across generations.

Avoiding the allure of passing trends is crucial in maintaining breed integrity. Ethical breeders resist the temptation to compromise standards for fleeting fads, understanding that enduring characteristics define the breed's identity and contribute to its sustained well-being.

Participation in dog shows is not merely a pursuit of recognition but a commitment to ethical representation. These shows provide a platform for breeders to showcase their adherence to standards, receiving valuable feedback that informs continuous improvement and maintains a high standard of excellence.

The responsibility of adhering to breed standards extends beyond the breeder's kennel. Ethical breeders prioritize educating puppy owners about these standards, empowering them to become advocates for responsible breeding and stewards of the breed's unique qualities.

Avoiding Genetic Problems

Ensuring the long-term health and well-being of a breed involves a dedicated effort to avoid genetic problems. Ethical breeders recognize the impact that genetics can have on the overall vitality of a lineage and undertake specific measures to mitigate potential issues.

- **Genetic Screening:** Ethical breeders prioritize comprehensive genetic screening for breeding dogs. This involves thorough testing for known hereditary conditions within the breed. By identifying potential genetic issues early on, breeders can make informed decisions about pairing dogs and work towards reducing the prevalence of such conditions.

- **Understanding Inherited Traits:** A deep understanding of inherited traits is fundamental to responsible breeding. Ethical breeders delve into the genetic history of their breeding dogs, tracing the inheritance patterns of specific traits and potential health concerns. This knowledge informs breeding decisions and contributes to the prevention of inherited problems.

- **Responsible Pairing Decisions:** Avoiding genetic problems requires responsible pairing decisions. Ethical breeders consider not only the physical attributes outlined in breed standards but also the underlying genetic factors. By selecting breeding pairs with complementary genetic profiles, breeders aim to reduce the likelihood of passing on hereditary issues to offspring.

- **Continuous Monitoring and Adaptation:** Ethical breeding is a dynamic process that involves continuous monitoring and adaptation. Responsible breeders stay informed about the latest developments in veterinary genetics and proactively adjust their breeding practices based on new insights. This commitment to staying current contributes to the ongoing improvement of genetic health within the breed.

- **Educating Puppy Owners:** An essential aspect of avoiding genetic problems is educating puppy owners. Ethical breeders provide information about potential genetic issues associated with the breed, offering guidance on preventative

measures and proactive health monitoring. This collabora-
tive approach ensures that puppy owners are well-equipped
to support the long-term health of their canine companions.

Understanding Dog Genetics and Breeding Pairings

Deciphering Genetic Complexity: At the heart of responsible
breeding lies a profound understanding of dog genetics. Ethical
breeders embark on a journey to decipher the genetic complexity
that shapes the traits, health, and behavior of their canine
companions. This comprehension is essential for making
informed decisions that contribute to the overall well-being
of the breed.

Inheritance Patterns: Ethical breeders delve into the intricacies
of inheritance patterns, unraveling how specific traits are passed
from one generation to the next. This knowledge forms the basis
for thoughtful breeding pairings, allowing breeders to predict
and influence the expression of desired characteristics while
minimizing the risk of genetic issues.

Genetic Diversity and Preservation: Maintaining genetic diversity is a key consideration in responsible breeding. Ethical
breeders strive to preserve the broad range of genetic material
within a breed, avoiding excessive inbreeding that can lead to
health issues. Thoughtful breeding pairings aim to balance
genetic diversity while adhering to breed standards.

Health Considerations in Pairings: Ethical breeders carefully
assess the health records and genetic backgrounds of potential
breeding pairs. This meticulous examination involves under-

standing any potential hereditary conditions and considering the overall health history of each dog. The goal is to promote pairings that enhance the health and vitality of the offspring.

Balancing Traits: Responsible breeding involves a delicate balance of traits. Ethical breeders consider not only the physical attributes outlined in breed standards but also behavioral traits that contribute to the well-rounded nature of the breed. This holistic approach ensures that breeding pairings contribute to the overall temperament and character expected from the breed.

Adaptation to Breed Standards: Ethical breeders leverage their understanding of genetics to adapt to evolving breed standards. As standards may change over time, responsible breeders incorporate new knowledge into their breeding practices. This adaptability ensures that breeding pairings align with the most current expectations for the breed.

Chapter 4

ESTABLISHING A HEALTHY BREEDING PROGRAM

Nutrition, Exercise, and Wellness

Venturing into the heart of responsible breeding, we discover that nourishing the essence of a healthy breeding program extends beyond mere pairings and pedigrees. It involves a harmonious dance of nutrition, exercise, and overall wellness—a dance that ensures the well-being of the enchanting canine companions central to our narrative.

The Potion of Optimal Nutrition: Picture a cauldron brewing with the essence of optimal nutrition. Ethical breeders, akin to skilled alchemists, understand the magical balance of nutrients that sustains their breeding dogs. A dash of essential elements, a sprinkle of portion control—this potion fosters the vitality and radiance of the breeding pack.

Crafting Wellness Plans like Ancient Scrolls: Each dog, a unique character in our mystical tale, deserves a wellness plan tailored to its individual journey. Imagine ancient scrolls adorned with personalized care rituals. Regular veterinary incantations, protective vaccinations, and preventive enchantments safeguard the well-being of each precious creature.

The Dance of Exercise and Energy: Envision a moonlit clearing where the dance of exercise unfolds. Ethical breeders orchestrate a balanced choreography, attuned to the energy levels of their dogs. A swirl of movement, a rustle of fur—this dance not only hones physical prowess but also nurtures a positive aura within the breeding sanctum.

The Alchemy of Body Condition: In the mystical art of breeding, body condition becomes an alchemical masterpiece. A vigilant watch over the corporeal realm ensures an optimal vessel for the magical act of reproduction. Maintaining the golden balance, breeders weave a tapestry of health that contributes to the vigor and longevity of their noble charges.

Guardians Against Overbreeding Shadows: Responsible breeders, akin to guardians of ancient wisdom, fend off the shadows of overbreeding. They comprehend the delicate dance between cycles, granting their breeding dogs the respite needed for recovery. A pause in the magical cadence, a moment of reprieve—this ensures the endurance of the breeding program.

Enchanting Minds with Mental Stimulation: Amidst the whispers of spells and enchantments, mental stimulation takes center stage. Ethical breeders, like wizards of cognition, infuse activities that captivate the canine mind. A symphony of engagement, a spell of enrichment—this preserves the mental well-being of the enchanted breeding pack.

Veterinary Care for Breeding Dogs

The Healing Sanctuaries: Veterinary Clinics: Imagine mystical sanctuaries, adorned with healing energies and the gentle hum of diagnostic instruments—the realms of veterinary clinics. Ethical breeders recognize these sanctuaries as havens of well-being for their breeding dogs. Regular pilgrimages to these healing domains become a ritual, ensuring that the enchanting companions receive the care they deserve.

Prophetic Check-ups: Peering into the Canine Future: Veterinarians, akin to seers, conduct prophetic check-ups that peer into the canine future. Ethical breeders understand the significance of these mystical consultations, where the health of breeding dogs is foretold. From comprehensive physical examinations to specialized tests, these check-ups unveil insights that guide breeders on the path of responsible stewardship.

Vaccination Spells: Shields Against Ailments: Vaccinations, cast as protective spells, create magical shields against the dark forces of ailments. Ethical breeders, custodians of these potent enchantments, ensure that their breeding dogs are shielded from the malevolent whispers of diseases. From puppyhood inoculations to booster spells, this magical immunization ritual fortifies the enchanting pack.

Healing Potions and Preventive Elixirs: In the apothecaries of veterinary wisdom, healing potions and preventive elixirs are brewed. Ethical breeders, apprentices of this mystical craft, administer these magical concoctions to ward off ailments and nurture robust health. From flea and tick potions to heartworm elixirs, these remedies weave a protective enchantment over the breeding dogs.

The Oracle of Genetic Testing: Unraveling the Canine Code: Genetic testing emerges as the oracle, unraveling the intricate code within the canine essence. Ethical breeders, seekers of truth, employ these mystical tests to peer into the genetic tapestry of their breeding dogs. This foresight allows them to navigate potential hereditary challenges and make informed decisions for the well-being of future generations.

Emergency Portals: Gateways to Urgent Care: Emergencies, akin to temporal disruptions, call for swift action through the gateways of urgent care. Ethical breeders, keepers of emergency portals, recognize the importance of immediate attention to injuries or sudden health crises. These portals, often in collaboration with trusted veterinarians, ensure that the enchanting companions receive timely and adept care.

Creating a Safe Breeding Environment

In the tapestry of responsible breeding, the environment where our enchanting companions dwell is not just a backdrop; it's the very canvas on which their well-being is painted. Creating a safe breeding environment is akin to crafting a haven, a sanctuary where health, happiness, and vitality flourish.

The Canvas of Cleanliness: Picture a canvas bathed in the hues of cleanliness. Ethical breeders understand that a clean environment is the foundation of well-being. From immaculate kennels to pristine whelping areas, this canvas sets the stage for a healthy breeding journey. Regular cleansing rituals become a pledge, ensuring that the breeding dogs dwell in spaces free from the shadows of contaminants.

Spatial Symphony: Designing Comfortable Abodes: The breeding environment is a spatial symphony where comfort takes center stage. Ethical breeders, akin to architects of canine comfort, design abodes that cater to the physical and emotional needs of their dogs. Spacious kennels, cozy whelping boxes, and outdoor areas for exploration compose the notes of this symphony, ensuring that the enchanting companions thrive in their living spaces.

The Breath of Fresh Air: Ventilation Alchemy: Fresh air, the invisible elixir, flows through the breeding sanctuary like a gentle breeze. Ethical breeders, conjurers of ventilation alchemy, ensure that the air within their breeding spaces is pure and invigorating. Adequate ventilation becomes the breath that sustains the enchanting pack, fostering an atmosphere of health and vitality.

Natural Illumination: Harnessing the Power of Sunlight: Natural illumination, the golden touch of the sun, bathes the breeding environment in warm radiance. Ethical breeders, appreciators of nature's gifts, harness the power of sunlight. Well-lit spaces not only create a visually appealing environment but also contribute to the physical and mental well-being of the breeding dogs.

Safety Enchantments: Warding off Potential Hazards: Safety enchantments are cast to ward off potential hazards that may lurk in the corners of the breeding sanctuary. Ethical breeders, protectors of the enchanting pack, conduct thorough safety inspections. From securing electrical wiring to eliminating toxic plants, these enchantments ensure that the breeding environment is a haven free from harm.

Whispers of Tranquility: Stress-Free Sanctuaries: Tranquility whispers through the breeding sanctuary like a soothing melody. Ethical breeders, conductors of stress-free environments, recognize the impact of a calm atmosphere on the well-being of their dogs. Whether it's minimizing loud noises or providing private spaces for rest, these gestures create a haven where the enchanting companions can flourish without the weight of unnecessary stress.

Chapter 5

RESPONSIBLE ADVERTISING AND MARKETING

Ethical Promotion of Puppies

In the realm of responsible breeding, promoting puppies ethically involves a set of practices aimed at establishing trust with potential owners. Here are key considerations for ethical puppy promotion:

1. **Authentic Representation:** Provide accurate and truthful information about each puppy. Share details about their lineage, health history, and living conditions. Authentic representation sets the foundation for trust between breeders and prospective owners.

2. **Transparency in Communication:** Openly communicate all relevant details, including health records, vaccinations, and any known genetic information. Transparency ensures that potential owners have a complete understanding of what to expect when bringing a puppy into their home.

3. **Clear and Honest Imagery:** Use clear and honest images of the puppies. High-quality photos that accurately repre-

sent the puppies' appearance and environment help build credibility. Avoid using exaggerated or misleading visuals in promotional materials.

4. **Educational Resources:** Provide educational content to prospective owners. This can include information about the breed, responsible dog ownership, and guidelines for puppy care. Educated owners are more likely to provide a suitable and loving home for the puppies.

5. **Qualifying Potential Owners:** Engage in conversations with potential owners to understand their living situation, previous experience with pets, and their commitment to responsible ownership. This screening process ensures that puppies are placed in homes that align with their needs and characteristics.

6. **Community Engagement:** Participate in community discussions about responsible breeding and dog ownership. Engaging with communities, both online and offline, helps build a network of trust. It also provides a platform for sharing experiences and knowledge.

7. **Referral System:** Establish a referral system where satisfied puppy owners can share their positive experiences. Word-of-mouth recommendations from happy owners can be a powerful ethical marketing tool.

8. **Clear Adoption Process:** Outline a clear and transparent adoption process. Clearly communicate the steps involved, from initial inquiries to the adoption day. A well-defined process helps manage expectations and builds confidence in potential owners.

9. **Follow-Up Support:** Offer ongoing support to puppy owners after the adoption. This can include guidance on training, healthcare, and general puppy care. Providing

support reinforces the breeder's commitment to the well-being of the puppies throughout their lives.

10. **Feedback and Improvement:** Welcome feedback from owners and use it for continuous improvement. Ethical breeders are open to constructive feedback, as it helps refine breeding practices and ensures a positive experience for both puppies and owners.

Building a Positive Reputation

Building a positive reputation as a responsible breeder is a multifaceted process that involves ethical practices, transparent communication, and a commitment to the well-being of both the dogs and their future owners.

Building a Positive Reputation:

1. **Ethical Breeding Practices:**

- **Breeding Standards:** Adhere to breed standards and prioritize the health and well-being of the dogs over quantity.
- **Genetic Health:** Implement responsible breeding practices to minimize genetic issues and hereditary conditions.
- **Limited Breeding:** Avoid overbreeding and give breeding dogs adequate time between litters to ensure their health and vitality.

1. **Transparent Communication:**

- **Openness and Honesty:** Communicate openly about your breeding practices, policies, and any known health information about the puppies.
- **Clear Contracts:** Provide detailed contracts that outline responsibilities for both the breeder and the new owner.
- **Availability:** Be accessible for inquiries and transparent in addressing concerns or questions from potential owners.

1. **Quality Care for Dogs:**

- **Health Checks:** Conduct regular health checks on breeding dogs and provide prompt veterinary care when needed.
- **Clean Living Conditions:** Maintain clean and safe living conditions for the dogs, ensuring their physical and mental well-being.
- **Nutritional Excellence:** Provide a balanced and nutritious diet tailored to the specific needs of each dog.

1. **Responsibility in Puppy Placement:**

- **Screening Process:** Implement a thorough screening process for potential owners, ensuring they are well-prepared for responsible dog ownership.
- **Matchmaking:** Match puppies with suitable homes based on the needs and characteristics of both the dog and the owner.
- **Post-Placement Support:** Offer ongoing support and guidance to new owners, reinforcing your commitment to the well-being of the puppies.

1. **Educational Outreach:**

- **Informative Resources:** Create and share educational content about responsible dog ownership, breed-specific care, and training tips.
- **Workshops and Seminars:** Conduct workshops or seminars to engage with the community, sharing your knowledge and expertise.
- **Breed-specific Information:** Provide detailed information about the breed's characteristics, exercise needs, and potential challenges.

1. **Community Engagement:**

- **Participation in Events:** Attend dog shows, community events, or breed-specific gatherings to connect with other breeders and potential puppy owners.
- **Online Presence:** Maintain a professional and informative website and actively engage on social media platforms to showcase your commitment to responsible breeding.
- **Networking:** Build positive relationships with local veterinarians, pet professionals, and other reputable breeders.

1. **Feedback Collection and Improvement:**

- **Solicit Feedback:** Encourage feedback from puppy owners and be open to constructive criticism.
- **Continuous Improvement:** Use feedback to continuously improve your breeding practices, communication methods, and overall customer experience.

1. **Legal Compliance:**

- **Adherence to Regulations:** Ensure compliance with local, state, and federal regulations related to dog breeding.
- **Transparent Pricing:** Clearly outline pricing structures, including any additional costs, to avoid misunderstandings.

1. **Positive Testimonials and Reviews:**

- **Encourage Reviews:** Request satisfied puppy owners to share positive testimonials and reviews.
- **Online Platforms:** Maintain a positive presence on online platforms, such as breed-specific forums and review websites.

1. **Crisis Management:**

- **Proactive Communication:** In the event of challenges or concerns, communicate proactively and transparently with affected parties.
- **Resolution Strategies:** Implement effective resolution strategies to address issues and maintain a positive reputation.

Developing a Strong Online Presence

In the ever-evolving landscape of responsible dog breeding, the digital space has become a vital canvas for breeders to convey their commitment, ethics, and the well-being of their beloved canine companions. Developing a strong online presence is not just a technological necessity; it's a heartfelt journey that involves transparency, education, and the art of connecting with those who share a passion for responsible pet ownership.

1. **Professional Website Development:**

- **Domain Name Selection:** Choose a professional and memorable domain name that reflects your breeding identity.
- **Mobile Responsiveness:** Ensure your website is optimized for mobile devices to provide a seamless user experience.
- **Clear Navigation:** Design an intuitive website with clear sections for breeding practices, information about breeding dogs, available puppies, and contact details.

1. **High-Quality Content Creation:**

- **Detailed Breeding Information:** Provide thorough details about your breeding practices, emphasizing ethical standards, health considerations, and your commitment to responsible breeding.
- **Educational Resources:** Create and share informative articles, blog posts, or resources that educate visitors about responsible dog ownership, breed-specific care, and relevant topics.
- **Visual Appeal:** Use high-quality images and videos to showcase your breeding environment, the well-being of your dogs, and the adorable nature of your puppies.

1. **Active Social Media Engagement:**

- **Platform Selection:** Choose social media platforms strategically based on your target audience. Platforms like Instagram, Facebook, and Twitter are effective for engaging content.

- **Consistent Updates:** Post regular updates about your breeding practices, upcoming litters, puppy milestones, and share engaging content related to dogs and responsible pet ownership.
- **Audience Interaction:** Respond promptly to comments, messages, and inquiries to foster a sense of community and trust.

1. **Online Networking and Community Building:**

- **Breed-specific Forums:** Participate in online forums and communities related to your dog breed to connect with other breeders, enthusiasts, and potential puppy owners.
- **Collaborate with Peers:** Collaborate with other responsible breeders and professionals in the pet industry to expand your network and share valuable insights.
- **Local and Global Engagement:** Engage with both local and global communities to broaden your reach and connect with diverse audiences.

1. **Search Engine Optimization (SEO) Strategies:**

- **Keyword Optimization:** Incorporate relevant keywords related to your breed, location, and breeding practices to enhance your website's visibility on search engines.
- **Quality Content for SEO:** Develop content that not only appeals to visitors but is also optimized for search engines, improving your website's ranking.

1. **Professional Branding:**

- **Logo and Brand Identity:** Create a professional logo and brand identity that visually represents your breeding program.
- **Consistent Branding Across Platforms:** Maintain consistent branding across your website, social media profiles, and any other online platforms.

1. **Testimonials and Reviews:**

- **Encourage Positive Feedback:** Request satisfied puppy owners to share testimonials and positive reviews about their experiences.
- **Display Feedback:** Showcase testimonials prominently on your website to build credibility and trust.

1. **Online Advertising Strategies:**

- **Targeted Advertising:** Utilize targeted online advertising on platforms like Facebook and Google to reach potential puppy owners.
- **Advertise Ethical Practices:** Highlight your commitment to ethical breeding in your advertisements to attract conscientious buyers.

1. **Regular Updates and Maintenance:**

- **Content Refresh:** Regularly update content on your website to reflect current practices, upcoming litters, and any relevant changes.

· **Technical Maintenance:** Ensure the technical aspects of your website, such as loading speed and security, are regularly maintained.

1. **Legal Compliance:**

· **Privacy Policies:** Clearly outline privacy policies on your website, detailing how you handle user data.
· **Compliance with Regulations:** Adhere to local, state, and federal regulations related to online activities, advertising, and data protection.

Chapter 6

LEGAL REQUIREMENTS AND REGULATORY COMPLIANCE

Understanding Laws for Dog Breeders

Understanding the legal requirements and regulatory compliance for dog breeders is a multifaceted journey that involves various aspects to ensure the ethical and responsible breeding of dogs. Let's navigate through the intricacies.

Licensing Requirements: Dog breeding operations are subject to licensing to ensure that breeders meet specific standards and regulations. The first step for any aspiring breeder is to research and obtain the necessary licenses from relevant authorities. This often involves submitting detailed applications, paying associated fees, and undergoing inspections to ensure that the breeding facility meets the required standards for animal welfare.

It's crucial to highlight that licensing requirements may vary based on the breeder's location. Some regions may have specific laws governing commercial breeding, while others may focus on the number of litters a breeder is allowed to produce annually. Researching and understanding the specific licensing requirements in your jurisdiction is paramount.

Breeding Standards: Maintaining high breeding standards is not only a legal requirement but also a moral obligation for responsible breeders. Breeders should familiarize themselves with the standards set by breed clubs, kennel clubs, or other relevant organizations. These standards often cover aspects such as conformation to breed-specific traits, genetic diversity, and overall health.

Ethical breeding practices involve selecting breeding pairs based on health, temperament, and adherence to breed standards. Breeders should strive to contribute positively to the breed by avoiding practices that compromise the well-being of the animals.

Health Regulations: Ensuring the health and well-being of both breeding dogs and their offspring is a fundamental aspect of legal compliance. Breeders are typically required to conduct health screenings for hereditary conditions, provide necessary vaccinations, and maintain regular veterinary care. Additionally, there are legal obligations regarding the documentation of health records and the disclosure of any known health issues to prospective buyers.

The sale and transfer of dogs also come under scrutiny, with regulations often stipulating the age at which puppies can be separated from their mothers and the information that must be provided to new owners. Transparent and ethical practices in health management contribute to the overall welfare of the animals and maintain the integrity of the breeding operation.

Ensuring Ethical Business Practices

Ethical practices form the bedrock of a reputable and responsible breeding business. Upholding transparency, honesty, and a commitment to the well-being of dogs and puppy buyers contributes not only to the success of your business but also to the overall integrity of the breeding community.

Transparency and Honesty:

Communication with Buyers: Transparency begins with clear communication. Potential puppy buyers should have access to comprehensive information about your breeding practices, health testing protocols, and the living conditions of your dogs. Openly discuss any challenges or limitations, ensuring that expectations align with reality.

Pricing Transparency: Transparency extends to the financial aspects of purchasing a puppy. Clearly outline the pricing structure, including what is covered in the cost and any additional fees. This transparency fosters trust and helps prospective buyers make informed decisions.

Responsible Advertising:

Accurate Representations: Your advertising materials should authentically represent your breeding program. Avoid exaggerations or misleading claims about the qualities of your dogs.

Authenticity builds trust and sets the foundation for a positive relationship with potential buyers.

Use of Images: Authenticity extends to the use of images. Utilize genuine photos of your dogs and facilities in promotional materials. This approach provides transparency and eliminates misconceptions that may arise from the use of stock photos.

Ethical Breeding Standards:

Adherence to Breed Standards: Strive for excellence in adhering to recognized breed standards. This not only preserves the integrity of the breed but also contributes to the overall health and temperament of your dogs. Engage in responsible breeding practices, avoiding any shortcuts that compromise ethical standards.

Avoiding Unethical Practices: Unethical practices, such as overbreeding or breeding unhealthy pairings, have long-term repercussions. Prioritize the well-being of your dogs over short-term gains. This commitment to ethical breeding practices ensures the creation of healthy, well-adjusted puppies.

Health and Well-being of Dogs:

Comprehensive Health Care: The health of your breeding dogs is paramount. Regular veterinary check-ups, vaccinations, and preventive care measures are essential. Prioritize a holistic approach to health care that considers both the physical and mental well-being of your dogs.

Comfortable Living Conditions: Provide your dogs with living conditions that prioritize their comfort and well-being. Adequate shelter, proper nutrition, and opportunities for socialization contribute to the overall happiness of your breeding dogs.

Customer Education:

Puppy Buyer Information: Educate potential buyers about responsible dog ownership. Provide detailed information about the specific needs and characteristics of the breed you are breeding. Equip buyers with resources that support them in providing the best possible care for their new companions.

Lifetime Support: Offer ongoing support to puppy buyers. Emphasize the importance of a lifelong commitment to the well-being of the dog. Providing resources, guidance, and a support network establishes a lasting relationship that extends beyond the initial purchase.

Incorporating these ethical practices into your dog breeding business not only positions you as a responsible breeder but also contributes to the positive reputation of the broader breeding community. By prioritizing transparency, responsible breeding standards, and the well-being of dogs and owners, you are not just running a business but actively contributing to the welfare of canine companions.

Chapter 7

DEVELOPING A COMPREHENSIVE BUSINESS PLAN

Financial Projections and Budgeting

E mbarking on a journey in dog breeding requires not only a passion for the well-being of your dogs but also a strategic approach to ensure the sustainability and success of your breeding business. Developing a comprehensive business plan, with a keen focus on financial projections and budgeting, lays the groundwork for a thriving and financially sound enterprise.

Business Plan Essentials:

Strategic Vision: Clearly outline the vision and mission of your dog breeding business. What are your long-term goals, and how do you envision contributing to the welfare of the breeds you work with?

Target Market and Niche: Identify your target market and niche within the dog breeding community. Understanding the demand for specific breeds or qualities can guide your breeding program and marketing strategies.

Competitor Analysis: Conduct a thorough analysis of competitors in your niche. What practices contribute to their success, and are there gaps in the market that your breeding program can uniquely fill?

Financial Projections:

Revenue Projections: Develop realistic revenue projections based on the expected number of litters, pricing strategy, and market demand. Consider factors such as the reputation of your breeding program and the desirability of the breeds you offer.

Expense Projections: Outline all anticipated expenses, including veterinary care, food, facilities maintenance, and marketing. Consider both fixed and variable costs to create a comprehensive overview of your financial commitments.

Breeding Program Investment: Assess the initial investment required for your breeding program. This includes acquiring breeding dogs, setting up suitable facilities, and investing in health testing and genetic screening.

Budgeting:

Operational Budget: Create a detailed operational budget that covers day-to-day expenses. This should include items such as food, grooming supplies, and routine veterinary care.

Capital Expenditure Budget: Plan for capital expenditures, including infrastructure improvements, equipment purchases, and any other significant investments. This budget ensures that you allocate resources for long-term sustainability.

Contingency Planning: Build a contingency fund into your budget to account for unforeseen circumstances or emergencies. This financial cushion provides stability during challenging times.

Financial Management Best Practices:

Record-Keeping: Implement robust record-keeping practices to track income and expenses accurately. This not only aids in financial management but also supports compliance with regulatory requirements.

Regular Financial Reviews: Schedule regular reviews of your financial performance against projections. Adjust your strategies based on actual outcomes to maintain financial health and make informed decisions.

Seek Professional Advice: Consider consulting with financial professionals, such as accountants or financial advisors, to ensure that your business plan aligns with sound financial principles.

Effective Marketing and Sales Strategies

Understanding Your Target Audience:

Demographic Analysis: Conduct a thorough analysis of your target audience. Understand their demographics, lifestyle, and preferences. Tailor your marketing messages to resonate with the specific needs and desires of potential puppy buyers.

Identifying Niche Markets: Explore niche markets within the dog-loving community. Identify segments that may be particularly interested in specific breeds or qualities. Tailor your marketing approach to appeal to these niche markets.

Building a Strong Online Presence:

Professional Website: Develop a professional and user-friendly website that serves as the central hub for your breeding program.

Ensure that it provides comprehensive information about your breeding practices, the health of your dogs, and available puppies.

Engaging Social Media: Leverage social media platforms to engage with your audience. Share captivating content, including photos and videos of your dogs, breeding practices, and success stories. Use social media as a tool to build a community around your breeding program.

Online Advertising: Consider targeted online advertising to reach a broader audience. Platforms such as Google Ads and social media advertising allow you to refine your targeting based on demographics, interests, and online behavior.

Utilizing Traditional Marketing Channels:

Printed Materials: Create high-quality printed materials, such as brochures and business cards, to distribute at local businesses, events, and veterinary offices. These materials should provide a snapshot of your breeding program and contact information.

Partnerships and Collaborations: Explore partnerships with local businesses, pet stores, or veterinarians. Collaborate on events or promotions that mutually benefit both parties and increase visibility within the local community.

Establishing Your Unique Selling Proposition (USP):

Highlighting Breed Qualities: Clearly articulate the unique qualities and characteristics of the breeds you specialize in. Your USP should convey why your breeding program stands out in terms of health, temperament, and adherence to breed standards.

Emphasizing Responsible Practices: Embrace responsible breeding practices as a core component of your USP. Highlight

41

your commitment to the health and well-being of your dogs, genetic testing protocols, and adherence to ethical breeding standards.

Sales Strategies and Customer Engagement:

Educational Workshops and Webinars: Host educational workshops or webinars on responsible dog ownership, breed-specific care, and the importance of choosing a reputable breeder. Position yourself as an authority in the field and engage with potential buyers.

Open House Events: Organize open house events where potential buyers can visit your facilities, interact with your dogs, and learn more about your breeding program. This personal touch enhances the connection between breeders and buyers.

Measuring and Adapting:

Analytics and Metrics: Implement tools to track the performance of your marketing strategies. Analyze website traffic, social media engagement, and the effectiveness of advertising campaigns. Use these metrics to refine your approach.

Feedback and Surveys: Seek feedback from puppy buyers and website visitors. Use surveys to understand their experience with your breeding program and identify areas for improvement. Incorporate this feedback into your ongoing marketing strategy.

Building a Positive Reputation:

Testimonials and Reviews: Encourage satisfied puppy buyers to provide testimonials or reviews. Positive feedback builds credibility and trust among potential buyers. Showcase these testimonials on your website and marketing materials.

Community Engagement: Actively engage with the dog-loving

community. Participate in forums, social media groups, and local events. Building a positive reputation within the community contributes to the success of your marketing efforts.

Effective marketing and sales strategies are not just about attracting buyers; they are about establishing lasting connections and a positive reputation within the dog breeding community. By understanding your audience, building a strong online presence, and emphasizing your unique selling proposition, you position your breeding program for sustained success.

Chapter 8

PUPPY CARE AND RESPONSIBLE OWNERSHIP

Prenatal and Postnatal Care for Breeding Dogs

E mbarking on the journey of dog breeding is a profound commitment, one that extends far beyond the arrival of a litter of puppies. Central to this commitment is the imperative to safeguard the health and well-being of both the breeding dogs and their precious offspring.

Prenatal Care for Breeding Dogs:

Nutrition and Supplements: Provide breeding dogs with a well-balanced and nutritionally rich diet, especially tailored to meet the specific needs of pregnant and nursing females. Consider consulting with a veterinarian to determine appropriate supplements to support the health of both the mother and developing puppies.

Regular Veterinary Check-ups: Schedule regular check-ups with a veterinarian during pregnancy. These appointments allow for monitoring the health of the mother, ensuring that she is in optimal condition to support a successful pregnancy and delivery.

Environmental Comfort: Create a comfortable and stress-free environment for pregnant dogs. Minimize exposure to loud noises, abrupt changes, or stressful situations. Provide a quiet and secure space where the expectant mother can rest and prepare for the upcoming birth.

Preparing for Whelping:

Whelping Box Setup: Set up a designated whelping box well in advance of the expected due date. The box should be spacious, easily accessible, and lined with clean and comfortable bedding. Ensure that it provides a secure and warm space for the mother and puppies.

Whelping Kit: Prepare a whelping kit containing essential supplies such as clean towels, sterile scissors for cutting umbilical cords, a heating pad, and a bulb syringe for clearing airways. Having these items readily available ensures a smooth whelping process.

Monitoring Temperature and Humidity: Keep a close eye on the temperature and humidity in the whelping area. Maintain a warm and stable environment to prevent chilling of the newborn puppies. Use heating pads or heat lamps as needed, ensuring that there are areas within the box where the temperature is adjustable.

Postnatal Care for Mother and Puppies:

Initial Health Check: Conduct a thorough health check of the mother and puppies immediately after birth. Ensure that all puppies are breathing well, have successfully nursed, and are free from any physical abnormalities. Address any concerns promptly with the assistance of a veterinarian.

Nutrition and Hydration: Continue providing a nourishing diet for the nursing mother to support milk production. Adequate hydration is equally crucial for both the mother and the puppies. Monitor the mother's weight and adjust her diet as needed.

Socialization and Interaction: Encourage positive socialization experiences for the newborn puppies. Gently handle and interact with them to promote early social development. This positive early exposure contributes to well-adjusted and confident adult dogs.

Health Monitoring and Veterinary Care:

Regular Veterinary Check-ups for Puppies: Schedule regular veterinary check-ups for the puppies to monitor their growth, development, and overall health. Keep a record of vaccinations, deworming, and any necessary preventive care.

Postpartum Check-up for the Mother: Schedule a postpartum check-up for the mother to ensure her recovery from the birthing process. Address any lingering health concerns or nutritional needs to support her well-being.

Educating New Puppy Owners:

Provide Comprehensive Care Guidelines: Offer new puppy owners a comprehensive care guide that includes information on feeding, grooming, training, and healthcare. Empower them with the knowledge and resources needed to provide the best possible care for their new canine companions.

Encourage Responsible Ownership: Emphasize the responsibilities of pet ownership, including the importance of regular veterinary visits, training, and socialization. Educate owners on the long-term commitment required to ensure the well-being of their dogs.

Socialization, Training, and Nutrition for Puppies

In the intricate tapestry of responsible dog breeding, our exploration now takes us into the pivotal domains of socialization, training, and nutrition for the burgeoning members of our canine community—the puppies. These fundamental facets form the bedrock upon which we sculpt the character, behavior, and well-being of these nascent companions, propelling them towards lives of fulfillment and harmonious coexistence with their human counterparts.

Socialization: Cultivating Well-Rounded Canine Citizens

Early Experiences:

- Introduce puppies to a diverse array of sights, sounds, and environments during their formative weeks. Familiarity with varied stimuli serves to instill confidence and resilience in the face of novel experiences.
- Facilitate positive interactions with individuals of different ages, laying the groundwork for the formation of trusting relationships beyond their primary caregivers.
- Gently expose puppies to other animals, fostering positive social behavior and preempting fear-based responses.

Positive Reinforcement:

- Implement positive reinforcement techniques to reinforce desirable behaviors. This approach not only bolsters obedience but also fortifies the bond between puppies and their human guardians.
- Arrange playdates with well-mannered adult dogs, fos-

tering appropriate social conduct and providing valuable learning opportunities.

Structured Socialization Events:

- Participate in structured socialization events, such as puppy classes or group walks. These environments offer controlled settings for interaction, enabling puppies to acquire crucial social skills.

Training: Forging Connections Through Positive Guidance
Basic Obedience Commands:

- Initiate early basic obedience training, imparting commands like sit, stay, and recall. Consistent, positive reinforcement fosters responsiveness and reinforces the profound bond between the puppy and their owner.
- Employ treats, praise, and play as rewards for commendable behavior, reinforcing the understanding that positive actions elicit favorable outcomes.

Behavioral Training:

- Address undesirable behaviors promptly and consistently using positive reinforcement methods. Redirecting attention and rewarding alternative behaviors can reshape conduct effectively.

Consistency and Patience:

- Approach training with unwavering consistency and patience. Dogs thrive on routine, and repetition of commands in various settings solidifies their understanding.

Nutrition: Nourishing the Foundation of Health
Balanced Diet:

- Provide a well-balanced and nutritionally complete diet tailored to the specific needs of growing puppies. Consult with a veterinarian to determine the most suitable dietary plan.
- Establish a regular feeding schedule, ensuring that meals are proportioned according to the age, size, and breed of the puppy.

Healthy Treats:

- Incorporate healthy treats into training sessions, promoting positive reinforcement while maintaining a balanced overall diet.

Monitoring Growth:

- Regularly monitor the puppy's weight and adjust their diet as needed to support optimal growth and development.

Identifying and Addressing Health Issues in Puppies

As stewards of the well-being of our canine companions, it is imperative that we navigate the realm of identifying and addressing health issues in puppies with diligence and care.

Vigilance in Health Observation:

- Conduct Regular Health Checks:
- Perform routine health checks, including observation of body condition, coat quality, and general demeanor.
- Monitor for changes in behavior, energy levels, and appetite, as these can be early indicators of underlying health issues.
- Watch for Digestive Health:
- Keep a close eye on digestive health, noting any signs of diarrhea, vomiting, or irregular bowel movements.
- Monitor for potential allergies or sensitivities to specific foods, adjusting the diet accordingly.

Common Health Issues in Puppies:

- Parasitic Infections:
- Regularly deworm puppies as per veterinary recommendations to prevent and address internal parasites.
- Implement preventive measures against external parasites, such as fleas and ticks.
- Respiratory Infections:
- Be attentive to symptoms of respiratory issues, including coughing, sneezing, or nasal discharge.
- Promptly seek veterinary attention if respiratory symptoms persist or worsen.

- Orthopedic Concerns:
- Monitor for signs of orthopedic issues, such as limping, difficulty in movement, or reluctance to engage in physical activities.
- Ensure that the living environment provides appropriate surfaces for puppies to prevent joint stress.

Early Intervention and Veterinary Care:

- Schedule Regular Veterinary Check-ups:
- Adhere to a schedule of regular veterinary check-ups to monitor overall health and address any emerging concerns.
- Discuss vaccination schedules and preventive care measures with the veterinarian.
- Immediate Response to Symptoms:
- Act promptly if any health concerns arise, seeking veterinary advice and intervention without delay.
- Follow prescribed treatment plans diligently, including medication administration and any necessary lifestyle adjustments.

Nutritional Considerations:

- Balanced Diet for Growth:
- Provide a nutritionally balanced diet that supports the specific needs of growing puppies.
- Consult with a veterinarian to ensure that dietary choices align with the breed, size, and age of the puppy.
- Adequate Hydration:
- Monitor water intake to ensure puppies remain adequately hydrated, especially during periods of increased activity or

warm weather.

Building a Holistic Health Approach:

- Mental and Physical Exercise:
- Encourage mental and physical exercise to promote overall well-being. Engage puppies in age-appropriate activities that stimulate both their minds and bodies.
- Emotional Health:
- Attend to the emotional health of puppies, fostering a secure and nurturing environment.
- Recognize the importance of positive social interactions with humans and other animals for their emotional development.

Educating New Puppy Owners

Being a new puppy owner is a thrilling adventure filled with joy, learning, and the formation of a lifelong bond. As you welcome your furry friend into your home, here are essential things to know to ensure a smooth transition and create a nurturing environment for your new companion.

1. Puppy-Proof Your Home:

- Safeguard your living space by removing potential hazards such as toxic plants, small objects, and electrical cords.
- Create a designated and secure area for your puppy to explore and relax.

2. Establish a Routine:

- Puppies thrive on routine, so establish a consistent schedule for feeding, playtime, potty breaks, and sleep.
- Be patient as your puppy adapts to their new surroundings and routine.

3. Nutrition Matters:

- Consult with your veterinarian to determine the best diet for your puppy's breed, size, and age.
- Follow a regular feeding schedule and avoid feeding your puppy human food, especially items that can be harmful to dogs.

4. Veterinary Care:

- Schedule regular veterinary check-ups to monitor your puppy's health and receive vaccinations.
- Discuss preventive care, spaying/neutering, and any concerns you may have about your puppy's well-being.

5. Training and Socialization:

- Start basic obedience training early using positive reinforcement techniques.
- Socialize your puppy to various environments, people, and other animals to promote well-rounded behavior.

6. Grooming and Hygiene:

- Establish a grooming routine that includes brushing, bathing, nail trimming, and dental care.
- Keep your puppy's living area clean to prevent the spread of bacteria and parasites.

7. Identification and Microchipping:

- Ensure your puppy wears a collar with an ID tag containing your contact information.
- Consider microchipping for an added layer of identification in case your puppy gets lost.

8. Play and Exercise:

- Engage in playtime and provide age-appropriate toys to keep your puppy mentally and physically stimulated.
- Gradually introduce short walks and other forms of exercise as your puppy grows.

9. Patience and Positive Reinforcement:

- Be patient and understanding as your puppy learns new behaviors and adapts to their surroundings.
- Use positive reinforcement, rewarding good behavior to strengthen the bond between you and your puppy.

10. Communication and Understanding:

- Learn to interpret your puppy's body language and vocalizations to understand their needs and emotions.
- Develop clear and consistent communication to facilitate

effective training.

11. Puppy Health Records:

- Keep detailed records of your puppy's health, vaccinations, and veterinary visits.
- Monitor your puppy's weight, growth, and overall well-being.

12. Create a Comfortable Space:

- Provide a cozy and secure space for your puppy to rest, whether it's a crate or a designated bed.
- Introduce your puppy to their designated area gradually, associating it with positive experiences.

13. Build a Strong Bond:

- Spend quality time bonding with your puppy through play, cuddles, and shared experiences.
- Understand and respect your puppy's individual personality and preferences.

14. Enjoy the Journey:

- Cherish the moments of joy and discovery as you and your puppy embark on this incredible journey together.
- Embrace the learning process, and celebrate the milestones and unique qualities of your new furry family member.

Chapter 9

ADDITIONAL CONSIDERATIONS AND RESOURCES

Choosing the Right Breed

While understanding and selecting the right breed is crucial for potential dog breeders, it also plays a pivotal role in the success and sustainability of a breeding business. Let's explore how the choice of breed intertwines with the dynamics of running a successful dog breeding enterprise.

Strategic Breed Selection: In the context of a breeding business, the choice of breed is not solely a personal preference but a strategic decision. Consider the market demand for specific breeds, the region you operate in, and the target audience you aim to serve. Identifying breeds with popular appeal can contribute to the marketability and profitability of your business.

Adaptability to Your Environment: Evaluate the adaptability of the chosen breed to your breeding facility and local environment.

Some breeds may thrive in specific climates or living conditions, and understanding these factors can impact the overall health and well-being of the breeding dogs and their offspring.

Health and Genetic Considerations: Prioritize breeds with strong health profiles and sound genetic backgrounds. This not only ensures the well-being of the animals but also contributes to the reputation and ethical standing of your breeding business. Regular health screenings and a commitment to responsible breeding practices are essential in this regard.

Market Trends and Preferences: Stay attuned to market trends and preferences in the dog breeding industry. Consumer preferences may shift over time, and being responsive to these trends can position your business for sustained success. Conduct market research to identify breeds that are currently in demand or emerging as popular choices.

Networking with Breed Enthusiasts: Engage with breed enthusiasts, fellow breeders, and relevant organizations within the dog breeding community. Attend dog shows, join breed-specific clubs, and participate in events where you can network with individuals who share a passion for the chosen breed. These connections can provide valuable insights and support for your business.

Ethical Breeding Practices: Regardless of the breed you choose, emphasize ethical breeding practices. Prioritize the health and welfare of your breeding dogs and their puppies. Maintain meticulous records, adhere to breed standards, and contribute to the preservation of the chosen breed's integrity.

Education for Potential Buyers: As part of your business strategy, consider incorporating educational content for potential buyers. Provide information about the chosen breed's characteristics, care requirements, and any specific considerations for responsible ownership. Educating buyers contributes to the creation of informed and responsible dog owners, reflecting positively on your breeding business.

Record-Keeping and Accounting Practices

Efficient and meticulous management of records not only ensures compliance with legal requirements but also provides valuable insights for strategic decision-making and the overall success of your breeding enterprise.

Comprehensive Record-Keeping: Establish a systematic approach to record-keeping that covers all aspects of your dog breeding business. This includes:

- **Breeding Records:** Maintain detailed records for each breeding pair, including pedigrees, health histories, and genetic information.
- **Litter Records:** Document information about each litter, such as birthdates, individual puppy details, vaccinations, and any relevant health observations.
- **Sales and Ownership Records:** Track the sales and ownership history of each puppy. Include details about the new owners, dates of transactions, and any contractual agreements.
- **Health and Veterinary Records:** Keep a comprehensive

record of veterinary visits, vaccinations, medications, and any health-related incidents or treatments.

· **Financial Records:** Document all financial transactions related to your breeding business, including income, expenses, and any investments made.

Legal Compliance: Ensure that your record-keeping practices align with legal requirements for dog breeders in your jurisdiction. This may include:

· **Licensing and Permits:** Keep copies of your breeding licenses and any required permits.
· **Sales Contracts:** Develop clear and comprehensive sales contracts for each puppy, outlining terms and conditions, health guarantees, and responsibilities of both parties.
· **Tax Records:** Maintain accurate financial records for tax purposes. Consult with a professional accountant to ensure compliance with tax regulations.

Utilizing Technology: Explore the use of technology to streamline your record-keeping processes. There are various software applications and tools designed for dog breeders that can help organize and manage breeding, health, and financial records efficiently.

Financial Management: Implement sound accounting practices to ensure the financial stability of your breeding business. This includes:

· **Budgeting:** Develop a realistic budget that encompasses all aspects of your business, from breeding-related expenses to marketing and administrative costs.

- **Revenue Tracking:** Clearly track and categorize sources of revenue, whether from puppy sales, stud services, or other income streams.
- **Expense Tracking:** Keep detailed records of all expenses associated with your breeding operation. This includes veterinary costs, breeding supplies, marketing expenses, and facility maintenance.
- **Profit and Loss Analysis:** Regularly analyze your financial statements to assess the profitability of your breeding business. Identify areas where costs can be optimized and revenue streams enhanced.

Risk Management: Anticipate and manage potential risks to your breeding business. This may involve:

- **Insurance:** Consider obtaining insurance coverage to protect against unforeseen events, such as liability insurance for potential legal issues or health insurance for breeding dogs.
- **Emergency Fund:** Maintain a financial reserve to address unexpected expenses or emergencies related to your breeding operation.

Collaborating with Professionals

Collaborating with professionals is a strategic move that can elevate the standards and success of your dog breeding business. Engaging with experts in various fields not only enhances the well-being of your breeding dogs and puppies but also contributes to the overall professionalism and credibility of your enterprise.

1. Veterinary Collaboration: Establishing a strong partnership with a reputable veterinarian is paramount for the health and welfare of your breeding dogs and puppies. Collaborate with a veterinarian who specializes in reproductive health and canine genetics. This collaboration should include:

- Regular health check-ups for breeding dogs.
- Pre-breeding health screenings to identify potential genetic issues.
- Guidance on vaccination schedules and preventive healthcare.
- Emergency and after-hours veterinary support.

2. Genetic Counseling: Consider collaborating with professionals specializing in canine genetics. These experts can provide valuable insights into:

- Genetic testing for breeding pairs to assess the risk of hereditary conditions.
- Guidance on responsible breeding practices to minimize the impact of genetic disorders.
- Strategies for maintaining genetic diversity within your breeding program.

3. Legal and Compliance Professionals: Ensure your dog breeding business adheres to local laws and regulations by collaborating with legal and compliance professionals. This collaboration may involve:

- Consulting with an attorney to create comprehensive sales contracts that align with legal standards.
- Staying informed about changes in legislation related to dog breeding.
- Securing proper licensing and permits for your breeding operation.

4. Marketing and Branding Specialists: To enhance the visibility and marketability of your breeding business, consider collaborating with professionals in marketing and branding. This may include:

- Developing a professional and user-friendly website to showcase your breeding program.
- Implementing effective social media strategies to reach a wider audience.
- Creating marketing materials that emphasize ethical breeding practices and the quality of your dogs.

5. Canine Nutritionists: Collaborate with canine nutritionists to ensure the optimal health and nutrition of your breeding dogs and puppies. This collaboration involves:

- Designing well-balanced and nutritionally sound diets for breeding dogs.
- Providing guidance on prenatal and postnatal nutrition for nursing mothers and growing puppies.
- Addressing any dietary concerns or special needs within your breeding program.

6. Professional Trainers and Behaviorists: For the well-rounded development of your puppies and to support new puppy owners, collaborate with professional trainers and behaviorists. This collaboration may include:

- Early puppy socialization and basic obedience training.
- Providing resources and guidance for new puppy owners on training and behavior management.
- Addressing any behavioral concerns or challenges that may arise.

7. Networking with Other Breeders: Collaborating with fellow dog breeders can be a valuable source of support and knowledge. This collaboration may involve:

- Participating in breed-specific clubs and organizations.
- Attending industry conferences and events to connect with other breeders.
- Sharing experiences and insights to collectively elevate breeding standards.

Staying Informed and Addressing Ethical Concerns

In the dynamic landscape of dog breeding, staying informed and proactively addressing ethical concerns are integral aspects that uphold the integrity of your breeding business. Remaining abreast of industry trends, best practices, and ethical considerations ensures that your breeding program not only meets but exceeds standards, fostering a reputation for responsible and ethical practices.

1. Continuous Education: Commit to ongoing education within the field of dog breeding. This involves:

- Regularly reading reputable publications, journals, and industry-specific literature.
- Participating in continuing education programs, webinars, and workshops related to canine genetics, health, and breeding practices.
- Networking with experienced breeders, veterinarians, and professionals to exchange knowledge and insights.

2. Breed-Specific Research: Conduct thorough research on the specific breeds you work with. This includes:

- Staying informed about breed standards and any updates or revisions.
- Monitoring health trends and potential genetic issues associated with the chosen breeds.
- Engaging with breed-specific organizations and resources to access the latest information.

3. Ethical Breeding Practices: Place a strong emphasis on ethical breeding practices, including:

- Adhering to breed standards and avoiding practices that compromise the health or well-being of the dogs.
- Prioritizing the overall welfare of your breeding dogs and their puppies throughout their lives.
- Implementing responsible breeding strategies that con-

tribute to the preservation and betterment of the chosen breed.

4. Open Communication with Puppy Buyers: Foster transparent and open communication with potential puppy buyers. This involves:

- Clearly outlining the breeding practices and standards followed in your program.
- Providing detailed information about the health and genetic background of breeding dogs and puppies.
- Offering support and guidance to new puppy owners on responsible ownership and care.

5. Ethical Advertising and Marketing: Ensure that your advertising and marketing strategies align with ethical principles:

- Avoid misleading or exaggerated claims about your breeding program or the qualities of your dogs.
- Provide accurate and honest information about the breeds you work with, including potential challenges or considerations.

6. Addressing Controversies: Be prepared to address controversies or ethical concerns that may arise within the dog breeding community:

- Respond promptly and professionally to any inquiries or concerns raised by fellow breeders, buyers, or the public.
- Demonstrate a commitment to ethical practices by actively addressing and resolving any issues that may arise.

7. Breed Preservation Efforts: Engage in efforts that contribute to the preservation and betterment of the breeds you work with:

- Support breed-specific rescue organizations and initiatives.
- Contribute to breed preservation projects that focus on maintaining genetic diversity and health.

8. Community Involvement: Participate in the broader dog breeding community to stay connected and informed:

- Attend industry events, conferences, and seminars to engage with professionals and enthusiasts.
- Join or contribute to online forums and discussions related to responsible dog breeding.

By consistently staying informed and actively addressing ethical concerns, you not only uphold the standards of your breeding program but also contribute positively to the broader dog breeding community.

CONCLUSION

As we conclude this comprehensive guide on dog breeding business for beginners, it's gratifying to reflect on the journey we've undertaken. The world of dog breeding is a dynamic and rewarding endeavor, but it demands a commitment to ethical practices, continuous learning, and a genuine love for the well-being of our canine companions.

Throughout these pages, we've delved into the intricacies of ethical breeding practices, responsible business management, and the multifaceted world of dog ownership. From defining the principles of ethical breeding to navigating the complexities of genetic health and breed standards, we've aimed to equip aspiring dog breeders with the knowledge and insights needed for success.

In the realm of business management, we explored legal requirements, financial considerations, and the vital role of marketing in reaching the right audience ethically. Understanding the responsibilities of dog ownership, from prenatal and postnatal care to promoting responsible ownership within the community, forms a cornerstone of our commitment to the well-being of the dogs we breed.

We navigated the nuanced terrain of collaboration with professionals, emphasizing the importance of partnerships with veterinarians, genetic counselors, legal advisors, and marketing specialists. By joining forces with experts in various fields, we elevate not only the standards of our breeding practices but also contribute to the broader community of dog enthusiasts.

The journey doesn't end here; it's an ongoing commitment to staying informed, addressing ethical concerns, and actively contributing to the preservation and betterment of the breeds we hold dear. As you embark on your dog breeding venture, remember that each decision you make has a profound impact on the lives of the dogs you care for and the families they become a part of.

May this guide serve as a valuable resource on your journey, offering insights, guidance, and inspiration as you navigate the intricate world of dog breeding. Whether you're just starting or have years of experience, the pursuit of excellence in ethical breeding practices remains a shared commitment that unites us as responsible stewards of our cherished canine companions.

Here's to a future filled with healthy, happy dogs, satisfied puppy owners, and a community of breeders dedicated to the welfare and preservation of our beloved breeds. As you turn the last page, consider it not an end but a beginning—a beginning of a journey that intertwines passion, knowledge, and responsibility in the wonderful world of dog breeding. If there are further questions or aspects you'd like to explore, the door is always open. Wishing you success and fulfillment in your dog breeding endeavors!